D1411926

Colors in Nature

Red

by Rebecca Stromstad Glaser

Bullfrog Books

Ideas for Parents and Teachers

Bullfrog Books let children practice reading informational text at the earliest reading levels. Repetition, familiar words, and photo labels support early readers.

Before Reading

- Discuss the cover photo. What does it tell them?
- Look at the picture glossary together. Read and discuss the words.

Read the Book

- "Walk" through the book and look at the photos. Let the child ask questions. Point out the photo labels.
- Read the book to the child, or have him or her read independently.

After Reading

- Prompt the child to think more. Ask: What red things do you see outside? Are they natural or man-made?

For my Mira, whose favorite color is red.
— RSG

Bullfrog Books are published by Jump!
5357 Penn Avenue South
Minneapolis, MN 55419
www.jumplibrary.com

Library of Congress Cataloging-in-Publication Data
Glaser, Rebecca Stromstad.
 Red / by Rebecca Stromstad Glaser.
  p. cm. -- (Bullfrog Books. Colors in nature)
 Summary: "This photo-illustrated book for early readers tells about plants and animals that are red and how colors work in the natural world. Includes picture glossary"-- Provided by publisher.
 Includes bibliographical references and index.
 ISBN-13: 978-1-62031-036-6 (hardcover : alk. paper)
 ISBN-13: 978-1-62496-040-6 (ebook)
1. Red--Juvenile literature. 2. Color--Juvenile literature. 3. Nature--Juvenile literature. I. Title.
 QC495.5.G586 2014
 535.6--dc23   2012039932

Series Editor   Rebecca Glaser
Book Designer   Ellen Huber
Photo Researcher   Heather Dreisbach

Photo Credits: Corbis, 17–18; Dreamstime, cover, 6–7, 8; Getty Images, 10–11, 18–19, 23tl, 23tr; iStockphoto, 4, 9, 12, 15, 22a, 22b, 23ml, 23mr, 23br; Shutterstock, 3b, 5, 13, 20, 21, 22c, 22d, 23bl, 23br; Superstock, 1, 14; Veer, 24

Printed in the United States of America at Corporate Graphics, North Mankato, Minnesota.
4-2013 / PO 1003

10 9 8 7 6 5 4 3 2 1

Table of Contents

Looking for Red

Where do you see red?
Look around in nature.

I see a ladybug.

Why is it red?

Red tells birds
that ladybugs
taste bad. Yuck!

I see a maple leaf.
Why is it red?

It changes color in fall.

I see a cardinal.
Why is it red?

The color comes from seeds it eats.

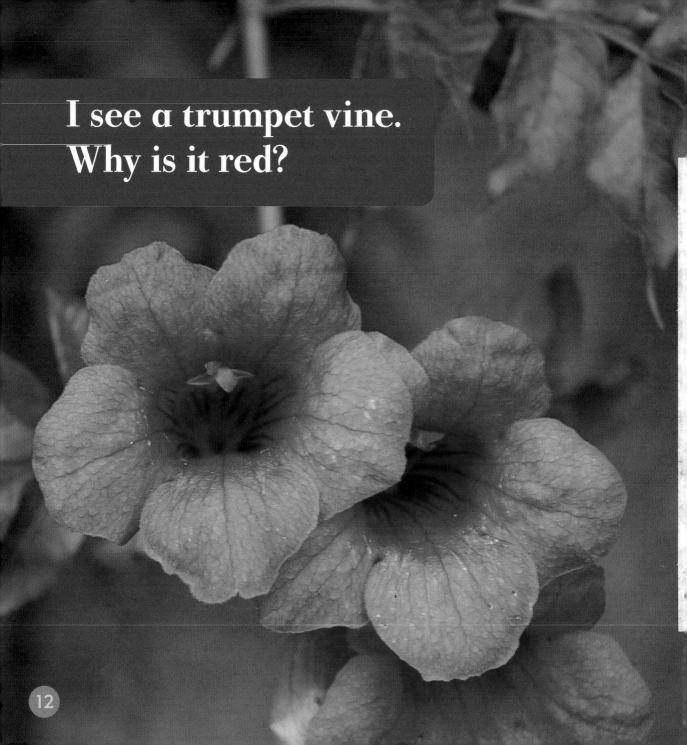

I see a trumpet vine.
Why is it red?

vine

Red helps hummingbirds find it.

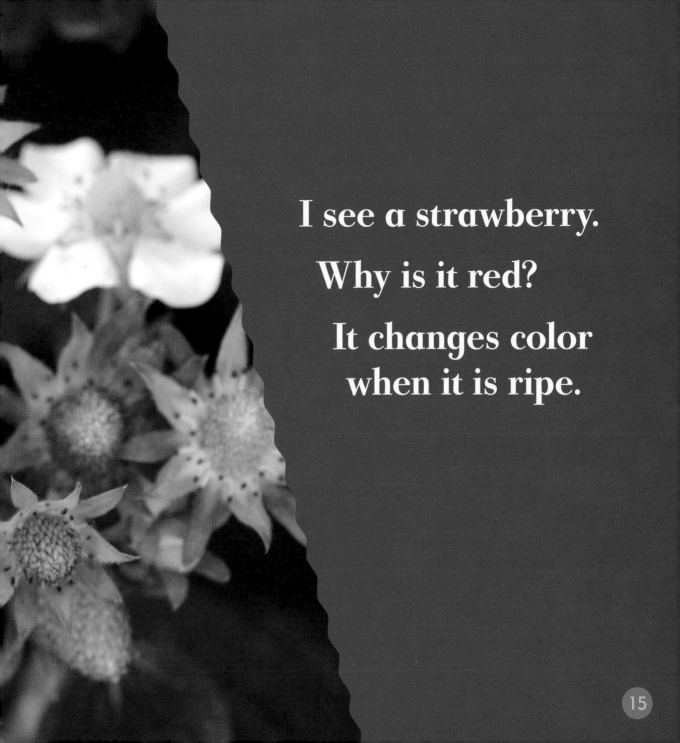

I see a strawberry.

Why is it red?

It changes color
when it is ripe.

I see a poison arrow frog.

Why is it red?

Red tells other animals the frog is poison!

I see a salamander.
Why is it red?

Red scares away animals that want to eat it.

I see a scarlet ibis.
Why is it red?
It eats red shrimp.

shrimp

What colors do you see in nature?

Shades of Red

coral

raspberry

tomato

ruby

Photo Glossary

cardinal
A bird that lives in North America; males are bright red and females are red-brown.

salamander
An animal with smooth, moist skin that looks like a small lizard.

maple
A tree that grows in North America; its leaves have five main parts.

scarlet ibis
A bird with a long curved beak that wades in the shores of warm oceans.

poison arrow frog
A frog that lives in the rain forest; its poison is used on arrows for hunting.

trumpet vine
A vine that grows in North America with red flowers shaped like trumpets.

Index

To Learn More

Learning more is as easy as 1, 2, 3.

1) Go to www.factsurfer.com

2) Enter "red" into the search box.

3) Click the "Surf" button to see a list of websites.

With factsurfer.com, finding more information is just a click away.